Nature Discoveries
with Uncle Mike

Birds
IN MY BACKYARD

MIKE ATNIP

ISBN: 978-1-941213-93-3

Cover photo: © shutterstock.com

All photographs in this book are by Mike and Daniel Atnip.

Printed in India

Published by:
TGS International
P.O. Box 355, Berlin, Ohio 44610 USA
Phone: 330-893-4828 | Fax: 330-893-2305 | www.tgsinternational.com

TGS001178

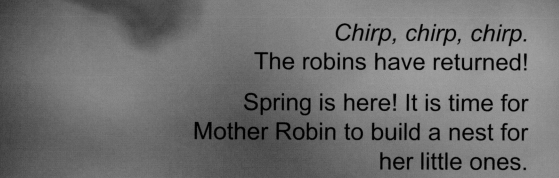

Chirp, chirp, chirp.
The robins have returned!

Spring is here! It is time for
Mother Robin to build a nest for
her little ones.

She often builds her nest in the fork of a tree.

Did you walk right past her without seeing her?
She will sit very quietly, peeking down at you.

Splish, splash!

Mother left the nest to quickly take a bath and grab a bite to eat.

While she is away, we will peek into the nest. Three blue eggs! Can you guess why there are only three?

6

Day by day Mother Robin keeps the eggs warm. If you come close, she will carefully watch you, hardly moving.

After about two weeks, the eggs hatch.
The babies are not very pretty, are they?
They are blind and totally helpless.

Soon Father
and Mother Robin
are busy bringing
the babies food.
The babies will
grow fast!

9

Within a few days, feathers start to appear and their eyes begin to open.

Not far away, another robin built a nest.
Maybe there will be cousins close by!

Life is easy for the babies.
They enjoy the beautiful days
of May while Father and
Mother Robin gather food.

Oh, no! Something has caught the mother of the other nest. Feathers are scattered close by. The eggs will not hatch.

Life is not always safe for baby robins. Raccoons, cats, hawks, and other animals will eat them. At night the baby robins huddle in the nest.

The nest is getting very full.
Now you can understand why
there were only three eggs!

Imagine how full this nest would be with six little birds! Some robin nests have that many.

17

Oh, look! Forty steps away in a cedar tree is another nest with five speckled eggs. Where is the mother? I hope nothing caught her. Can you guess what kind of birds these eggs belong to?

I try to feed the baby robins a worm. But I do not know how to feed them. The babies open their mouths, but when I drop the worm into one mouth, it slides right out and crawls away.

God taught Father and Mother Robin the right way to feed their babies. The bug must go deep into the throat! Both parents bring food and take trash away from the nest.

21

The time has come to leave the nest. It will be a few days before the babies can fly well, but they are gaining strength and will soon be flying like their parents.

The robin nest is empty. Look how
clean it is! Father and Mother Robin did
a good job of caring for their babies.
Soon the mother will be building a new
nest and raising another set of babies.

24

In the other nest, the eggs are hatching! Have you already guessed what kind of birds they are?

Blue jays! Only four of the five babies are left. They grow fast, like the robins. The nest would be really full if all five had lived.

The baby blue jays soon leave the nest. Father and Mother Blue Jay will still bring them food for several days until their feathers are large enough to fly.

Many other birds with bright colors share the backyard with the robins and blue jays. Let's look at some of them. Can you find all fourteen goldfinches that are feeding on this rainy day?

God made some birds red. The cardinal is almost completely red. He is watching us very closely. He is more nervous than the robins are.

This rose-breasted grosbeak munches on a sunflower seed.

The red-headed woodpecker has a full red head. Look how he uses his tail like a third leg.

The red-bellied woodpecker has only half a red head. Doesn't the baby look big enough to feed itself?

The hairy woodpecker has only a small red stripe on his head. He looks just like the downy woodpecker except he's bigger. Each woodpecker was designed by God.

The cedar waxwing has only a small red, waxy spot on each wing—and red juice on his beak and belly since he has been eating red berries.

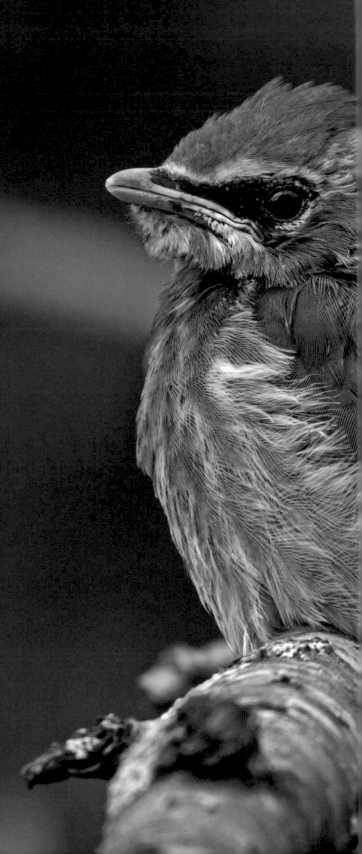

This cedar
waxwing baby
was also eating
red berries. It
does not have red
on its wings yet,
but it already has
the bright yellow
on its tail.

The eastern bluebird is blue like the blue jay. However, an adult bluebird will grow only as big as a baby blue jay that has just left its nest.

The rust-orange bib around the eastern bluebird's throat is the same color as the robin's belly.

The white-breasted nuthatch is also blue like a blue jay, but is much smaller. Nuthatches are the only birds that can climb down a tree headfirst!

Even though this song sparrow has
no red, blue, yellow, or gold on him,
he still sings praises to God.

It is now September, and the days are getting cooler. The baby robins are full-grown. Most of the robins will begin to fly south where more food is available in the winter. Goodbye, robins! Come again next year!

About the Author

Mike Atnip, his wife Ellen, and their son Daniel live in New Bedford, Ohio. Mike grew up among the cornfields of east-central Indiana, tromping through the fields and woods on a regular basis. Ellen grew up in southeast Pennsylvania, at the foot of Blue Mountain, but later lived in northern New York where the snow blows deep. Daniel was adopted from the tall Andes Mountains in Bolivia, South America, but has spent most of his life in the United States.

The Atnip family hopes that people young and old will see God's glory, power, and love in the creation of so many marvelous forms of life, and submit their hearts to Him as to a loving Father and Friend.

Mike welcomes reader response and can be contacted at atnips@gmail.com. You may also write to him in care of Christian Aid Ministries, P.O. Box 360, Berlin, Ohio 44610.

Christian Aid Ministries

Christian Aid Ministries was founded in 1981 as a nonprofit, tax-exempt 501(c)(3) organization. Its primary purpose is to provide a trustworthy and efficient channel for Amish, Mennonite, and other conservative Anabaptist groups and individuals to minister to physical and spiritual needs around the world. This is in response to the command ". . . do good unto all men, especially unto them who are of the household of faith" (Galatians 6:10).

Each year, CAM supporters provide approximately 15 million pounds of food, clothing, medicines, seeds, Bibles, Bible story books, and other Christian literature for needy people. Most of the aid goes to orphans and Christian families. Supporters' funds also help to clean up and rebuild for natural disaster victims, put up Gospel billboards in the U.S., support several church-planting efforts, operate two medical clinics, and provide resources for needy families to make their own living. CAM's main purposes for providing aid are to help and encourage God's people and bring the Gospel to a lost and dying world.

CAM has staff, warehouses, and distribution networks in Romania, Moldova, Ukraine, Haiti, Nicaragua, Liberia, and Israel. Aside from management, supervisory personnel, and bookkeeping operations, volunteers do most of the work at CAM locations. Each year, volunteers at our warehouses, field bases, Disaster Response Services projects, and other locations donate over 200,000 hours of work.

CAM's ultimate purpose is to glorify God and help enlarge His kingdom. ". . . whatsoever ye do, do all to the glory of God" (1 Corinthians 10:31).

Creation to Redemption

God created the birds on the fifth day and man on the sixth day. At first man lived in harmony with God and the earth. But after Adam and Eve sinned, some people began to worship the creation rather than the Creator. Others began to selfishly destroy the creation in their pursuit of money, pleasure, or fame.

But God sent His Son Jesus into the world to rescue us from our sin. Jesus taught us to abandon the idolatry of nature worship and to be good stewards of God's creation. He died on the cross and rose again so that we can be born again and enter the kingdom of God.

This kingdom of God is made up of those who have allowed Jesus to be King of their lives. Jesus leads these people into a harmonious relationship with God and teaches them to live holy, loving, and unselfish lives as they relate to people and things on this earth. They are in the world but not of the world and look forward to their final redemption in heaven.